COMING CLEAN

6 Steps to
MAKING AMENDS
With Your Body

PENNY PLAUTZ

WELLPOWER, LLC

DISCLAIMER

THIS BOOK IS DESIGNED to provide information for those interested in improving their relationship with their body. It is sold with the understanding that the publisher and the author are not engaged in rendering medical information. The author is not a doctor, a nutritionist, or a registered dietician. The information she provides is based on her personal experience as a Certified Eating Psychology Coach.

The information does not take the place of professional medical advice. The author does not claim to cure any condition or disease. The author and publisher expressly disclaim responsibility to any person or entity for any liability, loss, or damage caused or alleged to be caused directly or indirectly as a result of the use, application, or interpretation of any material provided to you as the reader.

This is for educational and informational purposes only. The publisher and author cannot and do not guarantee that you will attain a specific or particular result, and you acknowledge that results differ for each individual. Health, fitness, and nutrition success depends on each individual's background, dedication, desire, and motivation. As with any health-related program or service, your results may be different and will be based on many variables, including, but not limited to, your individual capacity, life experience, unique health and genetic profile, starting point, expertise, and level of commitment.

CONTENTS

Here I am, coming clean,
willing to tell the truth
and reconcile
my relationship
with my body.
Whatever I've been
telling myself
up until now
is just a story.
It's time to write
a more empowering one.
It starts with this
love letter to my body.
My hope is that you will write one
to your body too.

Penny Plautz

WHY MAKING AMENDS MATTERS

IF YOU'VE STRUGGLED in your relationship with your body, if your body has ever let you down, if you have dealt with chronic pain or serious illness, if weight or body image issues have plagued you throughout your life, the last thing you may want to do is write a love letter to your body.

But since you are reading this, I suspect you've stumbled upon a certain truth: your relationship with your body impacts every other relationship you have.

Think about it. If you don't feel good about the way you look, feel, or function, you try to hide, minimize, or excuse your body for its alleged imperfections. When you do this, you cannot be fully present. Part of you will always be deflecting, defending, or diverting the energy and attention running through you, to you, or for you.

This is exhausting. It chips away at your confidence and your well-being. It erodes your relationship with others. When you are always protecting yourself, people are not able to access the part of you that is authentic, engaged, relaxed, or spontaneous. And neither are you.

You may tell yourself you will step up and stand in your power when something external happens. You'll be happy when you weigh a certain amount, look a specific way, perform better than you have before, gain more experience, earn more credentials, have more money, or … (fill in the blank).

But that's a game you won't win. The closer you get to your goal, the more elusive it becomes. The ten pounds you thought would make you feel fabulous become fifteen. The bachelor's degree you earned starts to feel meaningless without a master's degree. Even if you exceed your yearly goal in commissions, next quarter's need to be higher. Keeping success and happiness in the future, one step removed from where you are now, reinforces the idea that neither you nor your efforts will ever be quite enough.

You can choose to feel courageous, confident, and complete just as you are right now. But you may be unwilling to do so. Making amends with your body can feel futile. Believing you are broken can make healing seem improbable. Why pursue something impossible?

Here's why. Your desire to investigate this idea, to read this book, suggests that part of you is yearning to expand and open yourself to healing. This may be true even as another part of you is trying to contract and stay safe. It's human nature to contract just before your life is about to expand.

Because your body is the part of yourself that the world can see, judge, and compare to other bodies, it's easy to blame for a lot of things. And you can usually find someone to agree with you. How many times have you asked, *"Does this outfit make me look fat?"* And whatever answer you received, you heard, *"Yes. Absolutely."*

You can gather evidence to support any hypothesis you put forth. Why not gather evidence of your brilliance, creativity, or unique contributions?

While you may think having the "perfect" body will lead to love and acceptance, perfection takes its toll in time, energy, and money. Attaining, maintaining, and sustaining a flawless face, buxom bosom, bodacious backside, lean legs, flat stomach, white teeth, fabulous hair, and perky attitude takes a village. It also takes an unlimited beauty budget, serious willpower, and all of your free time.

In addition to that, perfection doesn't guarantee a happily ever after. At best, it may lead to temporary infatuation, and at worst, to unrelenting control. In most cases, the pressure of perfection just makes people irritable and edgy.

Most people don't relate to perfection. But they do relate to the quirks, cracks, and alleged broken bits you are afraid of showing. These are the qualities that make you utterly adorable and heartbreakingly human. What makes you lovable is not what people see on the outside but what they see *inside of you.*

As a certified eating psychology coach and fitness professional for over thirty years, I can tell you that everyone's relationship with their body is complicated. Even people who appear to be in excellent shape endure needless suffering in their exhausting efforts to maintain impossible standards of beauty and perfection.

MY STORY

For as long as I can remember, my relationship with my body has been tumultuous. I was anorexic before anyone understood what that was or how to treat it.

As a fitness instructor, people constantly critiqued my physique. I believed my weight equaled my worth, putting my self-esteem on shaky ground. Even as I ventured into the worlds of education and coaching, my standards for success were always predicated on my being fit and healthy.

But when the pandemic hit, I began a free fall into uncertainty, shock, and disbelief.

I had just returned from a retreat in Bali, where I experienced profound body-based healings. Breathwork, shamanic dance, daily massages, and ceremonies with Balinese healers had reacquainted me with my body. Because of the intense heat and humidity, I'd spent most of my time in a swimming suit and sarong in or near the water, and this attire quickly brought my body image issues to the surface for me to face and ultimately release.

Fortunately, I was surrounded by fellow coaches and healers who were not afraid to dive deep and get to the subconscious issues that were running the show and shaping my story. Issues that had plagued me for a lifetime were finally loosening their grip on me. I was excited to share these breakthroughs when I returned to the States.

But the world had changed while I was gone. As I tried to process the new world order, Bali became a distant memory. Life in lockdown consisted of trying to save the world one day and checking out completely the next. I began comforting myself with coffee cake, chocolate chips, and any "forbidden foods" that I'd previously considered off-limits. *If the world's ending,* I rationalized, *I might as well eat whatever I want.*

My body responded by packing on the pounds. COVID-19 became code for the amount of weight I gained. As an eating psychology coach, I understood what was going on and even why. I felt hopeless to do anything about it and ashamed that I'd lost the will to practice what I preached.

None of the strategies I'd previously used to lose weight were working, and I started to feel desperate. Exercising more and eating less—*a dubious strategy to begin with*—wasn't working. This added insult to injury; not only was I not nourishing my body with healthy, whole foods, I was making it work harder.

HATING MY WAY TO A BODY I LOVED WAS CLEARLY NOT WORKING.

I had a choice. I could continue to let my relationship with my body torment me, or I could allow it to show me where life was asking me to grow and expand.

Bali sparked the realization that I could have a different kind of relationship with my body. However, it would require a new strategy based on coming clean and accepting my body on its terms.

That meant listening to it. Being okay with it, no matter how much I weighed, how ashamed I felt, or how hopeless my health situation seemed. It meant learning to nourish my body, monitor my thoughts, feel my emotions, and support my spirit.

This was no easy task. What often happens when I indulge in unhealthy habits over time is my brain stops communicating properly with my body. Because of this, I knew I needed a different kind of help—something I'd never tried before. I needed a pattern interrupt—a way to reset my programming and detoxify my mind, body, emotions, and spirit.

I signed up for a health restoration, lifestyle modification program called SHAPE ReClaimed. It's designed to help balance brain chemistry, reduce inflammation in the body, detoxify, build up immunity, and release excess weight. Taking dietary supplement drops and following the nutrition protocol for thirty days helped me find my way back to feeling good in my own skin.

This experience led me to realize what an incredible teacher my body has always been. Even though I couldn't wrap my head around what was happening in the pandemic-ridden world, my body was feeling it and doing its best to process the stress and uncertainty. The doubt and self-loathing that came with the weight gain taught me to look for healthier ways to deal with feeling out of control.

Because I felt better as soon as I started cleansing and got results quickly, I became a SHAPE practitioner. This allowed me to add SHAPE ReClaimed products to my *Coming Clean Coaching Program* and help others reconnect with their bodies and sense of well-being.

My experience told me that focusing solely on the physical steps to help clients reach their goals would only get them so far. **For clients to sustain their success, they would need to get in touch with the beliefs they held about their bodies that kept their patterns in place and prevented permanent change.**

To help them do this, I had my clients write a love letter to their bodies. But before I could ask them to do this, I had to come clean and write one myself. This was a game-changer for me.

If you have the courage to write a love letter to your body, it can be a game-changer for you as well. You'll be seeing your body through the lens of love and experiencing it with curiosity and genuine appreciation instead of criticism, comparison, or contempt, maybe for the first time. When I wrote my love letter to my body, I discovered the profound power of telling the truth about my body, to my body, and listening to its response.

In this book, I'll show you how to do the same. I'll walk you through the six-step process I call **Making AMENDS** that will help you write the letter your body has been waiting a lifetime to read.

Facing a blank page can be intimidating, but following this step-by-step guide will help prime the pump and get your ideas, impressions, and inspiration flowing. I chose the acronym AMENDS as a way to make the process easy to remember.

The six steps in the **Making AMENDS** process are:

A = **Acknowledge Your Relationship with Your Body**

M = **Make Amends with Yourself and Others**

E = **Examine Your Expectations**

N = **Name and Claim, Navigate and Negotiate**

D = **Declare Your Intentions**

S = **See It and Sign**

Each step is an opportunity to collect data, gather input, elicit insights, and open yourself up to your body's perspective. Not all of this information will find its way into your final letter, but it's a great place to begin examining your experiences.

You may want to read all the way through this book first and then schedule quiet time to work through the questions at the end of each chapter.

Find a schedule you can commit to that gives you time to reflect on the questions and space to let the answers reveal themselves to you. They may show up in snippets of a conversation you overhear, lyrics to a song you suddenly can't get out of your head, or remnants of a reoccurring dream.

One thing that is crucial when answering the questions and writing your letter is to be in your body. So many people live mainly in their heads. Are you one of them?

I don't blame you for not wanting to drop down into what feels like enemy territory. But refusing to pay attention to and acknowledge what's going on in your body cuts you off from an incredible source of information. Your sensory systems receive an enormous amount of intel, most of it instantly and automatically. You may not even be aware of it.

But what if you were? And what if you could harness that energy and information?

By giving yourself a few minutes to be in your body, you become conscious of what is often unconscious. This provides you with an intimate experience of your subject matter … YOU!

To access some of my favorite techniques to help you be in your body, check out the Embodying Wellness video on my website at **www.comingcleancoaching.com**. From conscious breathing and tapping to shaking and snapping, I offer several simple moves you can do anywhere and anytime to help you feel grounded and centered in your body.

Don't worry if you feel silly when you first try these movements. It may have been a while since you've allowed yourself to really feel what it's like to be in your body. By engaging your body and your brain, you are gaining deeper access to the energy and information stored in your physical form.

Another way to engage your body is to record yourself asking the questions at the end of each chapter so you can hear yourself asking them in your own voice. **This engages your vocal cords and activates the power of your voice.** You can download a free voice recording app such as Dolby to do this. Then write down your answers in your journal.

You can also do the inverse. Read the questions in this book and speak your answers into a recording device. When you play back the recording, listen for what you did not say as well as what you did say. You may be able to pick up more information than you would by writing, *especially if you tell yourself you can't write.*

You can also record both the questions and your answers. You'll want to be sure to write down what you hear in your recorded responses to use in your love letter. Sometimes it's easier to do hard things, like writing a love letter to your body, in the company of others who are exploring the same subject. Processing the feelings these questions evoke in a group where you feel safe and seen can help everyone heal. A group can also provide accountability to actually write your letter.

If participating in a group appeals to you, **I invite you to join my Making AMENDS online community**. I facilitate this process in a variety of formats throughout the year. I'd love to have you as a part of our sacred community. To check out the schedule, visit **www.comingcleancoaching.com**.

For now, let's dive in.

CHAPTER ONE

STEP 1:
A = ACKNOWLEDGE
YOUR RELATIONSHIP
WITH YOUR BODY

STEP 1 ACKNOWLEDGES who you are and establishes what kind of relationship you currently have with your body. If you don't know where to start, consider one of two approaches: starting with the facts, or starting with gratitude.

To start with the facts, begin with physical things, like your name, age, height, weight, hair color, shoe size, or address, then move on to more complicated facts like your medical history, relationship status, or genealogy.

This may or may not have anything to do with what ultimately goes into your love letter. It does, however, get you moving your pen across the page, sending your fingers flying across the keyboard, or speaking your story aloud. It gets you in motion.

Once in motion, you can venture into untamed territory and ask questions about what makes you who you are. *What do you believe, what makes your day, what lights you up, what sends you over the edge, what stops you in your tracks, what have you never dared to admit—even to yourself?* This is your chance to come clean and set the story straight.

Getting up to speed on what is happening in your relationship with your body usually requires a bit of backstory. You may believe you know that story better than anyone, but writing it from your current perspective may yield unexpected insights.

It might also bring up emotions. Let them come. Give them room. Be gentle with yourself. No judgment necessary.

Although you may remember experiences in a certain way, stay open to other interpretations or impressions. Memory is a slippery thing. Your memories may be locked in at the age you experienced them, when you may have felt it was not safe to question your story. But now you may feel strong enough to dig deeper. You may have information you didn't have before or be able to put things in a different context.

If you don't want to start with the facts, **start with gratitude**. Assuming you are already aware of what you believe is "wrong" with your body, why not explore all that is "right" and absolutely exquisite about your body?

For example, every minute of every day, your body is carefully coordinating infinite efforts that you seldom acknowledge. Your heart beats a bit faster when you're thrilled or threatened, your digestive system metabolizes your meals, your ears pick up the emotional nuances in someone's voice, your skin registers the slightest change in temperatures … you get the picture. This is where you get to be grateful for all your body does to keep you alive and well.

HERE ARE QUESTIONS TO ASK YOURSELF AS YOU WORK THROUGH THIS SECTION:

What has been the greatest point of contention in my relationship with my body?

_____

_____

_____

How does my body get my attention?

_____

_____

_____

What has caused me the most grief or anguish?

_____

_____

_____

What has been a gift or a godsend about my body?

_____

_____

_____

Have I been plagued with health concerns, chronic pain, weight issues, or body image issues?

_____

_____

_____

Am I dealing with or have I dealt with an
eating disorder, a physical handicap, or a
life-threatening illness?

_____

_____

_____

How have these things shaped me?

_____

_____

_____

How may they have served me?

_____

_____

_____

How would I like my relationship with my body to be different?

_____

_____

_____

What am I grateful for about my body?

_____

_____

_____

What does my body do for me every day that I don't even think about?

_____

_____

_____

How is my body like that of my mother, father, sister, brother, grandmother, grandfather, aunt, or uncle?

_____

_____

_____

How much of my ancestry or heritage accounts for how I define myself?

_____

_____

_____

CHAPTER TWO

STEP 2:
M = MAKE AMENDS
WITH YOURSELF
AND OTHERS

HOW DO YOU MAKE AMENDS? How do you work through what feels unforgivable to you or beyond your ability to reconcile? What about when you are the one who needs forgiveness or reconciliation?

Step 2 is where you make amends for what others did to you or what you did to yourself or others. If you have a tried-and-true method you like to use, this is where to put it into practice. Maybe for you it's confession or confiding in a friend. Maybe it's scream-ing into a pillow. Maybe it's writing things down and burning them.

If none of these appeals to you, I recommend starting with the Ho'oponopono Prayer, an ancient Hawaiian healing practice of forgiveness. I discovered this practice through the work of Dr. Joe Vitale and Dr. Hew Len. According to Wikipedia, the Ho'oponopono Prayer is used to "*make things right, to correct, revise, rectify*" through "*prayer, discussion, confession, repen-tance, and mutual restitution and forgiveness.*" If it interests you, I encourage you to research it in greater depth.

For me, the power of this prayer lies in its simplic-ity. Four phrases repeated over and over can allow me to acknowledge my innocence and guilt. To acknowl-edge my misperception, my failure to understand, my desire to make things right, and my willingness to reconcile.

The four phrases of the Ho'oponopono Prayer are: **I'm sorry. Please forgive me. I love you. Thank you.**

Forgiveness is courageous work. Please be espe-cially kind to yourself throughout this step and seek out support if you need it.

HERE ARE QUESTIONS TO ASK
YOURSELF IN THIS SECTION:

What am I sorry for?

_____

_____

_____

How easy or difficult is it for me to forgive or attempt to reconcile a situation?

_____

_____

_____

Who or what would I like to forgive and/or be forgiven for?

_____

_____

_____

What do I believe is unforgivable?

_____

_____

_____

What is lovable about me?

_____

_____

_____

Can I see my own innocence?

_____

_____

_____

What has an unforgivable situation made me aware
of that I'm now grateful for?

_____

_____

_____

How hard is it for me to admit I've made a mistake or
to forgive myself for making mistakes?

_____

_____

_____

From whom did I learn about perfection?

_____

_____

_____

How often do I expect myself to be perfect?

_____

_____

_____

Whom do I like to blame for the way things are?

_____

_____

_____

How often do I take the blame for something?

_____

_____

_____

CHAPTER THREE

STEP 3:
E = EXAMINE YOUR EXPECTATIONS

IN MY EXPERIENCE, whenever I'm disappointed, devastated, or otherwise inconsolable, it's because my expectations were not aligned with the reality of my situation. Somewhere along the line, I didn't connect the dots between my actions and my expectations.

In Step 3, you have the opportunity to look at where your expectations may have gone awry.

You have hopes, dreams, and expectations about your body. When you can articulate what these are, whether they are realistic or not, you can start to understand why you may be feeling the way you do about your body.

For example, you may have thought you'd inherit the slender build of your Aunt Sophie but instead came from the sturdy stock of your Uncle Mort. You may have hoped you'd have a healthy childhood, running wild with the kids in your neighborhood instead of being cooped up with a breathing machine to manage your asthma. You may have thought dabbling in drugs was a harmless way to fit in, not realizing you could be doing irreparable damage to your body and brain.

In this step, you admit what your expectations are now, what they might have been before, how they have impacted your happiness, and how they affect the kind of relationship you have with your body.

HERE ARE QUESTIONS TO ASK YOURSELF IN THIS SECTION:

What have I expected from my body?

_____

_____

_____

How has my body measured up to my expectations?

_____

_____

_____

When did my body meet or exceed my expectations?

_____

_____

_____

When did my body let me down?

_____

_____

_____

Was there a time when things went horribly wrong with my body?

_____

_____

_____

Are my expectations realistic or achievable? Were they in the past?

_____

_____

_____

What do I expect of myself as I age? How is my body changing?

_____

_____

_____

Whose great expectations was I attempting to live up to?

_____

_____

_____

How has my body surprised me with its resilience?

_____

_____

_____

How has illness impacted my body?

_____

_____

_____

How did my body change after having children (if applicable)?

_____

_____

_____

BEFORE WE GO ON, I ASK YOU TO DO THREE THINGS:

Remember that your relationship with your body impacts every other relationship you have. Doing this work matters. Every question you are willing to answer will help you heal or reveal something you may not have been willing to look at before. Write down an affirmation of your worth and keep it in front of you as you go through the Making AMENDS process. For example:

"I love and respect my healthy body."

"My body is my oldest friend and dearest companion. I honor it with nourishing foods and loving thoughts."

"I love this new relationship I am creating with my body."

If you haven't already, watch the Embodying Wellness video at www. comingcleancoaching.com. This short video of simple three- to five-minute moves will help you get out of your head and into your body. You'll return to the questions with a whole new perspective.

Share this book with a friend. If you know of someone who struggles with their relationship to their body, please share this book with them. So many of us suffer in silence, feeling unnecessary shame around our bodies, unconsciously punishing them by withholding our love. Let's break that cycle by sharing this message of self-love.

CHAPTER FOUR

STEP 4:
N = NAME AND CLAIM, NAVIGATE AND NEGOTIATE

YOUR RELATIONSHIP WITH YOUR BODY up to this point may not have been ideal. **In Step 4, you get to Name and Claim the relationship you would like to have with your body, starting today.** This means you'll be navigating the ever-changing emotional terrain of new territory. You are essentially initiating a do-over, so there will be things to negotiate.

You will also establish non-negotiables in the new relationship with your body. You may have put up with behaviors in the past that have no business in this new way of treating yourself and allowing others to treat you. Writing down these behaviors and actions will help to anchor them in your awareness, enabling you to name and claim your new way of being in relationship with your body.

HERE ARE QUESTIONS TO ASK
YOURSELF IN THIS SECTION:

Where can I be flexible?

_____

_____

_____

Where do I stand my ground?

_____

_____

_____

What have I learned from the past that I can use now to craft a relationship with my body that is worthy of my respect, trust, and support?

_____

_____

_____

How does this compare with the relationship I've always imagined I could have with my body?

_____

_____

_____

Who do I need to become to create this kind of relationship with my body?

_____

_____

_____

What new behaviors or actions can I commit to now?

_____

_____

_____

How can I move, rest, and nourish myself in a way that feels supportive and nurturing?

_____

_____

_____

What are my non-negotiables? For example, "*I talk to myself with love and respect*." "*I nourish myself with healthy foods and healthy thoughts*." "*I always have my own back*."

_____

_____

_____

How might my intuition inform and assist me?

_____

_____

_____

What practices can I establish to keep myself on track?

_____

_____

_____

What is the best way for me to integrate new beliefs
and incorporate healthy habits?

_____

_____

_____

What is my wildest dream for my body?

_____

_____

_____

How might I claim some small part of that dream
today?

_____

_____

_____

When and where might I be tempted to fall back into old habits?

_____

_____

_____

CHAPTER FIVE

STEP 5:
D = DECLARE YOUR INTENTIONS

WHEN YOU COMMIT to another person, you agree to follow spoken and unspoken vows. This allows you to trust each other and develop a relationship built on mutual respect and shared goals. The same is true with your relationship to your body. You may have broken many promises to yourself in the past. This is your chance to renew your vows and commit to yourself.

In Step 5, you consciously and creatively declare how you intend to move forward in your relationship

with your body. Just like it may have taken you a while to compose your wedding vows, your commencement address, your retirement speech, or a winning sales pitch, declaring your intentions and crafting your vows to yourself may take time. This declaration of intention acts like your personal GPS, reminding you of who you are committing to become as you forge this new relationship with your body.

HERE ARE QUESTIONS TO ASK YOURSELF IN THIS SECTION:

What have I always hoped for or wished were possible in my relationship with my body?

_____

_____

_____

Am I aligning more with who I am becoming or who I was?

_____

_____

_____

What immediate actions can I take to improve my mood and support my well-being?

_____

_____

_____

What would I wish or intend for a beloved friend or family member?

_____

_____

_____

How do I remind myself I am enough and worthy of all I desire?

_____

_____

_____

In what situations am I most likely to abandon myself or break a promise to myself?

_____

_____

_____

What patterns do I need to be aware of that can sabotage my best intentions?

_____

_____

_____

What plans can I put in place to support myself when things get challenging?

_____

_____

_____

What scares me, and how can I constructively self-soothe?

_____

_____

_____

What will it take for me to commit to myself now?

_____

_____

_____

What has changed that makes me believe I can create
a new relationship with my body?

_____

_____

_____

CHAPTER SIX

STEP 6:
S = SEE IT AND SIGN

AS LONG AS YOU ARE ALIVE, you have the opportunity to evolve into a newer, truer version of yourself. Trust in your ability to manifest what's best for your entire being by seeing it in your mind's eye as already done. Seal the deal by signing. **Step 6 is where you see your new relationship with your body as already manifested.** Your signature amplifies the power of your words and intentions.

Is anything left unsaid? Write it down. Get it all out on paper. Say what you need to say. You've waited a long time to express and hear these things. Please don't miss your chance to tell the truth about yourself to yourself.

HERE ARE FINAL QUESTIONS TO ASK YOURSELF:

What words have I waited a lifetime to hear?

_____

_____

_____

Can I give myself the gift of these words?

_____

_____

_____

If I trust that no one else will see these words, what can I finally admit to, acknowledge, or unleash?

_____

_____

_____

What words can finally set me free?

_____

_____

_____

What has been left unsaid?

_____

_____

_____

What else?

_____

_____

_____

Is this true?

_____

_____

_____

Is this kind, respectful, and worthy of my attention?

_____

_____

_____

Am I holding anything back? If so, why?

_____

_____

_____

Can I see this as already manifesting?

_____

_____

_____

Can I allow something even better to happen?

_____

_____

_____

Am I willing to set the power of these promises to myself in motion by signing my letter?

_____

_____

_____

CHAPTER SEVEN

WHERE RESISTANCE LIES

OKAY. Now that you've done your research, it's time to give writing this love letter a try. Although you can use a computer, try to write the first draft longhand. **There is something magical about moving the ideas from your head through your heart to your hand and onto the page.**

Wait, what?

The magic is not flowing through you?

Words are failing you?

Despite working through the entire Making AMENDS process, you don't know where to begin or how?

The blank page or the empty screen is mocking you?

Don't panic. **This is what resistance looks like.**

Resistance is a normal response to what feels like an overwhelming expectation, like preparing your taxes, scheduling a dental procedure, or learning to quiet your mind. It's bound to show up now that you are coming face to face with so many things you haven't wanted to acknowledge.

Even though you've made it this far and convinced yourself now is the time for reckoning, some part of you would still rather resist than persist with this line of questioning and self-care.

The key to continuing on this quest is to discover where resistance lies and to coax it out into the open where you can see it for what it is.

Having additional support might be what you need to get you through the resistance. You may break through it when you decide to join my online Making AMENDS community to get access to videos and additional support for your love letter. You can find all the details at **www.coming-cleancoaching.com**.

For now, let me clue you in to sneaky places where resistance lies.

"I DIDN'T SIGN UP FOR THIS"

Whether you love or hate your body, it is the sacred container you call home in the physical world. But if you aren't sure you want to be in the physical world in the first place, any attempts to improve your relationship with yourself can feel pointless or temporary at best.

I understand. Planet Earth can be a difficult place to reside—*especially during a global pandemic*. Depression, isolation, loss, and despair can take up residence where there once was hope, delight, and opportunity.

It gets even trickier if your body feels like a battleground. This may be the case if you are fighting chronic pain, a debilitating illness, devastating loss or prognosis, hereditary condition, injury, accident, or anything that makes you feel different or unacceptable. When your body is a source of trauma or shame, all you want to do is escape.

Clearly, this isn't what you had in mind when you signed up for the human experience. You were hoping to experience the ecstasy of being in a body, not relentless suffering. You were longing for the pleasure of human connection, not self-isolation and social distancing.

You definitely did not sign up for the scenario you find yourself in.

And still, here you are.

If you've found your way to these words, I'm going to suggest that you did sign up for this. *Maybe in your enthusiasm to incarnate, you forgot to read the fine print where you assumed the risks inherent in being human.* You knew you had something to contribute. Gifts to share. Hearts to heal.

You knew it could be challenging. **You also knew you were equal to the task.**

Battling with your body makes it harder to get out of your own way and move forward with your mission. Decide now to be present and show up fully for yourself. This healing process will demand your full cooperation and participation. No more asking, "*Why bother?*" when you know precisely what's at stake.

In the words of intuitive energy healer Lee Harris, "*You can see the wound or you can be the wound.*" When you choose to see and heal your wounds, you enable yourself to help heal others.

"I'M A LOVER, NOT A WRITER"

I hear it all the time. *"It's easy for you to write a letter, Penny. You're a writer. But what about me? I can't write!"*

Saying you can't write a love letter because you're not a writer is like saying you can't take a selfie because you're not a photographer. Just as all you need for a selfie is yourself, **all you need to write a love letter is love.**

Writing something that can make you feel raw and vulnerable can be terrifying. Confessing love to anyone at any time takes courage. But remember, **this letter is for your eyes only**. It's all between you and the page. No one is going to judge you on your spelling, grammar, use of profanity, hyperbole, or anything else, for that matter.

This is your letter to your body. It's nobody's business but yours. You get to say whatever you want, however you want. *As long as you do not bash, abuse, blame, or shame yourself.*

Use your own voice. Use language that makes sense to you. Don't try to be anyone or anything other than a compassionate witness to whatever wants to reveal itself to you. If you swear like a sailor, write like a swearing sailor. If you're an editor or English teacher, follow all the rules of grammar and usage.

The truth is *you are the only one who can write this*

love letter to your body. Because you are the only one who knows what it's like to be you.

"I'M NOT READY"

Start before you're ready. The challenge of not knowing what you don't know will always be there. You won't know until you start. Catching yourself off-guard and surprising yourself with your ability to focus on and follow your fascination can be exhilarating.

If you truly weren't ready to begin this journey of reconnection and reconciliation, you wouldn't be reading this. **The courage that got you this far can carry you through the rest of this process.** You've already done the heavy lifting. Your job now is to acknowledge what you've done, what you've learned, where you might want to course correct, and what you'd like to create.

You can trust your body to keep you safe throughout this process. Your body is wired to protect you. If the line of questioning gets too intense, you will instinctively shut down. If this occurs, notice and be curious about when and where it happens. *This process will never ask you to bully or badger yourself into going where you're not ready to go yet.*

Trust what wants to be expressed. If there are tears, let there be tears. If there is anger, let there be anger. If there is laughter, let there be belly laughs. When you realize how long some of these emotions have been in lockdown, you can begin to understand what a courageous and liberating experience you are undertaking.

Emotions won't kill you. They just want you to experience and express them. **Once you allow yourself to feel them, you and your emotions are free to evolve.** It's when you stifle them that the situation gets ugly.

This process takes as much time as you need it to. It can take six hours, six weeks, or six months to go through the six steps. As you change, so will your relationship with your body.

That being said, don't let this become one of those activities you start but never finish because you want to get it right. There is no *"getting it right."* There is just coming clean and telling the truth as you've experienced it.

You've made it this far. You've never been more ready than right now.

THE RUT OF WRONGDOING:
"I'M UNWORTHY"

Your body always has been and always will be on your side, devoted to your survival. Would understanding this help you make peace with it? If you can't forgive your body, yourself, or the world at large, this creates a major roadblock to reconciliation.

When you feel unworthy of forgiveness, you insist the story you are telling about yourself is true, perpetuating a cycle of self-inflicted punishment. This is where coming clean and getting at the truth from another perspective can free you of unnecessary shame and guilt.

Could there have been a reason you starved yourself throughout high school or binged and purged your way through college? Was it really your fault you were attacked? Were you really to blame for the abuse you endured? Was it your fault you lost your baby or couldn't conceive a child? Were you to blame for breast cancer?

It's hard to do the work of forgiveness alone when you're convinced of your guilt. If you can, I recommend seeking out a coach, counselor, clergy person, or someone trained in forgiveness work to help you find evidence of your innocence. If the story you've been telling yourself has insisted that you serve a life sentence, then doing this work may set you free.

Your body registers every insult, injury, hurt, or humiliation in the moment and attempts to tuck them safely away, hoping that by ignoring them, they will go away once and for all.

But they don't. Whenever you are in doubt, these wounds shout at the top of their lungs. Whenever you attempt to do something bold and brave, they try to protect you by reminding you of *what could happen* by remembering what did happen.

Even if it was long ago and time has distorted the details, these old, questionable interpretations become the gospel on which you base your current actions.

This is where writing a love letter to your body can catapult you out of the rut of wrongdoing. By confronting the truth of the situation, you acknowledge that you survived. You have, in fact, lived to tell about it. Once you can come clean and tell the truth, no matter how difficult or damaging, you can begin to heal.

How you choose to tell the story is up to you.

I encourage you to write your love letter to your body as part of your newer, truer story. **Transforming your relationship with your body into one of respect, trust, and love is a gift only you can give yourself.** It starts with your willingness to let your body tell its side of the story.

CHAPTER EIGHT

PUTTING IT ALL TOGETHER

NOW THAT YOU'VE GONE THROUGH the six steps to Making AMENDS and faced your resistance, you are ready to start writing.

This is your moment of truth. This is where you transition from researching to writing and making your love letter a tangible document.

It's like preparing a feast for your family and friends. First, you commit to the challenge, knowing that preparing a feast will expand your culinary capabilities. Then you decide on the menu. You research recipes and make sure you have the ingredients for each dish. You gather the groceries and supplies you need. You mix, measure, prep, and proceed to pull the meal together.

Peripheral considerations like the presentation, timing, and pairing of the food and beverages also require your attention, as do conversational landmines and contingency plans for keeping your guests comfortable. Far more work goes into facilitating your successful soirée than you originally imagined. You accept the challenge, knowing the experience will illuminate things within yourself that you didn't know you contained.

And so it is with your love letter. Who you become in the process of Making AMENDS and learning to love yourself will give you a greater appreciation for your capacity to love.

It may take several attempts before you officially start, *let alone complete*, your love letter. Keep at it. Come back to the process and allow the pen to move across the page. You'll get there.

Here's a tip for when you're tired of trying: *You don't always have to go the extra mile.* **Sometimes, you just need to go the extra quarter-mile.** Sometimes, going just a little above and beyond what you believe is possible for you is all you require.

I did not design this to be a daunting task. **It's meant to be a fun, fascinating, and life-changing adventure.** Kind of like parenting or running a business.

Once you've completed the first draft of your letter, you'll most likely want to edit, revise, rearrange, and rewrite. No worries. **This is a living, breathing document.** You get to tweak, edit, add, and subtract as much or as little as you want.

As I mentioned before, **this love letter is for your eyes only.** You may eventually want to share your letter with others if you believe it will help them heal. But initially, if you write your letter for someone else to read, you'll censor yourself and won't go as deep, be as honest, or touch on the truths that have the potential to transform your relationship with your body.

My hope is that you will fall in love with yourself in the process of writing this letter. That you will remember all the things that are lovable, outrageous, unique, and even unmentionable about you and find them worthy of your own admiration and respect.

It's my belief that when you fall in love with another person, you simultaneously fall in love with yourself. As your hidden talents, quirks, and vulnerabilities reveal themselves to another, they reveal themselves to you as well.

As Rumi said, *"Lovers don't finally meet somewhere. They're in each other all along."*

You may be so focused on your imperfections that you fail to see that others are standing in awe, marveling at your magnificence.

Writing this letter is your opportunity to remember that you are made of miracles and magic. It's time to own your throne and claim your inheritance.

Write on!

P.S. Once you've written your letter, you will most likely experience a fierce temptation to rip it up or burn it. Please don't. It is a sure sign you've done some serious reconciling. **Congratulations on completing this process!**

If you'd like to be a part of our Coming Clean love letter writing community and receive regular doses of inspiration, sign up here and download "5 Tips for Coming Clean": **www.comingcleancoaching.com**.

I'd love for you to email me at penny@well-power.com and tell me when you've written your letter so I can celebrate with you.

P.P.S. In the next chapter, I share the letter I wrote to my body. I hope it inspires you to write your own love letter to your body. I promise it will be worth it if you do.

CHAPTER NINE

DEAR BODY, I CAN EXPLAIN ...

I HAVE BLAMED SO MANY THINGS on you, Dear Body. **So many ways I have shamed you and used you as an excuse not to show up and be fully present.** To not be me, the full expression of who I am—*quirky, creative, compassionate, wise, weird, woo-woo, funny, fabulous, daring, and different.*

I had this ridiculous notion that if I had the perfect body, I'd have the perfect life. **That somehow my weight equaled my worth.** That if my body was deemed acceptable to others, I might be able to accept it myself.

But I had it all backward.

The love and acceptance had to start with me. I had to know that I mattered regardless of how I chose to interpret what I saw in the mirror on any given day.

So, I'll start with the Hawaiian practice of forgiveness and reconciliation, the Ho'oponopono Prayer (discussed in Chapter Two). This is where all negotiations begin with me. **I'm sorry. Please forgive me. I love you. Thank you.**

You, Dear Body, have always been an incredible teacher. Despite my attempts to control every little detail, you have always overridden my "*authority*" with your undeniable truth. The harsher the terms, the bigger the pushback on your part. And rightly so. You were, after all, tasked with keeping me alive at all costs.

You know me inside out. My oldest friend, my most loyal and faithful companion, **you have never stopped working for me in all these years.** No matter how many times I gave you reason to.

You have worked tirelessly on my behalf in ways I'll never completely comprehend.

You've made sure my heart beats, my body heals, my senses interpret incoming data at a phenomenal rate and adjust accordingly, my organs function, my cells communicate, you eliminate toxins, digest food, extract nutrients, distribute energy, allocate oxygen, protect my brain, defend my immune system, and the list goes on.

My health, well-being, and survival have been your #1 priority 24/7 for my entire life.

For that I am eternally grateful.

And yet I have withheld so much love, so much pleasure, so much joy from you. There is no excuse for such stinginess.

I would never treat a friend or even a complete stranger with the total disregard and disrespect with which I have treated you. I have held you to impossible standards and punished or dismissed you when you refused or were physically incapable of complying with my demands.

I have blamed and shamed, starved and stuffed, ridiculed and criticized, betrayed and abandoned you time and again. That's a strange way of showing my appreciation and gratitude.

Please forgive me.

I know you have registered and recorded every wrongdoing, every insult, injury, compromise, or transgression somewhere in my cells. **What's most appalling is that the majority of these wounds were self-inflicted.**

After all these years, **I still have these outrageously unrealistic expectations about how you should look, feel, perform, and age.**

For some reason, I expect you to be able to **easily attain and effortlessly maintain the elusive ideal weight** etched on my driver's license. I expect the thick, lustrous hair I was supposed to inherit from my paternal grandmother to be on my head, not my chin. And I expect any extra *"insulation"* to go where it's needed, not where it's already been.

How can I expect to look, feel, and weigh the same as I did years ago when I was teaching fitness classes twice a day, swimming all summer, rollerblading around the park, and dance parties were the norm? Not the menopausal melodramas, midlife mayhem, or pandemic paranoia that are the new normal now.

Life feels heavier these days. And so do I.

It's not only unrealistic, it's unkind for me to not allow you, Dear Body, to evolve and expand into all you've become. **You are a living landscape of love, loss, and longing. Of dreams, daring adventures, and disappointments.**

Why would I resent the way those experiences frame my face, burrow into my belly, settle on my shoulders, huddle around my hips, and linger on my legs?

But sometimes I do.

I rail against a reality that made me feel invisible at forty and obsolete by fifty. I know I have a choice whether to buy into this or not. Just as I know feeling fabulous at fifty, sixty, seventy, eighty, and beyond is its own kind of revenge against an ageist, sexist society.

I resent being held to a standard of beauty defined by an industry that sells us all on the notion that **we are fundamentally flawed, inadequate, and in constant need of fixing because we will never be enough on our own.**

Of course, **nothing could be further from the truth.**

Yet, sadly, being bombarded with this message most of my life shaped my relationship with you, Dear Body. **I began to believe them, which meant distrusting you.**

Forgive me. I had a lapse in judgment.

Was that when the insidious voice of "*reason*" convinced you to act your age? And insinuated you're too old to ride a bike, take up skiing, or attempt a cartwheel and the splits?

When did *"reason"* take over for the sassy seeker of truth who knows that **life truly begins when the Princess becomes the Queen and decides to Own Her Throne?**

Feeling fat, fuzzy, or fatigued is no way to reclaim the health, power, or joy that is yours for the taking. **It's just a temporary response to an untenable situation.**

I understand how world events leave you feeling weary. **I know how very sensitive you are, Dear Body,**

and how you feel the world's pain acutely. I also know how hundreds of tiny hurts collect around your heart, a heart hoping to heal but reluctant to forgive or forget.

I understand how the silent suffering and shame of our ancestors lives on in you. I feel how the belly, breasts, birth canal, and back bear the burden of betrayal, bravery, and being powerfully intuitive, witchy women.

Boldness is your birthright. **To transcend the limitations of our mystical mothers and give voice to their deepest truths is your promise to them, Dear Body.** A tall order indeed.

Padding and protecting yourself in defense is a reasonable response. Seeking solace in comfort food and drinks, numbing out with Netflix, or nonstop work is a familiar fix for troubling times. **But it also creates a pattern of powerlessness and self-loathing**. Of becoming an internal terrorist who criticizes and condemns you for not being able to handle it all without gaining weight and losing yourself.

It's easier to give up on deep connections and true intimacy than to drop down into you, Dear Body, to seek a solution. Exposure to that kind of emotional intensity and vulnerability can feel overwhelming.

You are not to blame for the abuse you endured. **You paid the ultimate price of nice.** First through anorexia, then promiscuity, then disconnecting from joy, personal power, and the soul's insistence on forgiveness.

Learning to instinctively trust and align with your wisdom has never been quick or easy. It has taken decades and several failed attempts to reconcile my relationship with you.

But it is the only way forward. **Because you, Dear Body, hold the key to me.** You are the ongoing mystery my mind can't unravel. You honor the unspoken truths my heart can't bear to witness. You evolve with every breath.

So here we are. *Coming Clean* **once again.** Reclaiming our health, power, and joy—one truth at a time.

HERE ARE MY NEW VOWS TO YOU.

Dear Body, I promise to nourish you, honor you, and respect you.

1. I will feed you delicious, nutritious foods and provide chocolate on demand.

2. I will drink water all day even if it means ten more trips to the toilet.

3. I will allow you to rest, relax, and follow your own rhythm.

4. I will move you in ways that strengthen, stretch, challenge, and delight you.

5. I'll adorn you with your favorite bling. *Including your most fabulous shoes.*

6. I'll put you in water when you get cranky. *I'll even throw in flippers and your favorite flowered swim cap.*

7. I'll make play part of each day and let pleasure be the measure of our success.

8. I'll consider aging as a gift and observe the changes with curiosity and kindness, grace and gratitude, humility and hilarity.

9. I promise to be present with you *in this moment*. I will not compare you to younger, thinner, healthier, or sexier versions of yourself or others.

10. I will drop down into you and access your immense emotional intelligence when I feel frightened or freaked out. Numbing out is *no longer* an option.

11. I will ask for your assistance in inter-preting and clarifying your cryptic clues to our physical, mental, emotional, and spiritual well-being.

12. I will come clean and tell your truth for the health of all concerned.

You, Dear Body, are an exquisite vehicle for the expression of my hopes and dreams. And I so seldom acknowledge you, thank you, or tell you I love you.

You met the exact physical specifications required for me to learn my life lessons this time around. **You have never failed to do your job and provide life-supporting feedback.**

Even if my grievances against you felt justified at the time, **I know you always have been and always will be on my side.**

At long last, I'm listening. Help me interpret every ache and every pain, the weight loss and weight gain. Help me hear the wisdom in my gut, the who-when-where-why-what, and the truth you convey in your very nuanced way.

I am paying attention. **What I require now is the courage to consistently show up, honestly address your concerns, and consider your requests.**

Fear-based thoughts are just the story I default to when I'm "hangry," lonely, tired, or scared. **I'm ready to write a more empowering story and be free of the not-so-civil war I've allowed to wage within me for far too long.**

I'm not saying I will never again blame you for all my issues. And I'm fairly certain skinny jeans and other questionable trends will never be a fashion choice *we* make.

But I will love you, nevertheless. Because I couldn't do any of this without you. I need all parts of me aligned and accounted for in order to carry out my mission: *for all bodies to feel they belong and are accepted here.*

It starts with me. Let me end where I began.

I'm sorry. Please forgive me. I love you. Thank you.

And so it is. **It is already done.** And our new relationship has begun.

Penny

CHAPTER TEN

LET'S KEEP THE CONVERSATION GOING

YES! You want to write a love letter to your body.

It's a lovely idea.

You can clearly see how going through this process will unlock a world of wisdom and be the breakthrough you've been waiting for.

You also know yourself well enough to know that, left to your own devices, your love letter will never see the light of day.

Not if you attempt to go it alone.

You need accountability.

I understand.

The good news is **you don't have to do this alone**.

HERE ARE WAYS WE CAN WORK TOGETHER.

1. You can check my website **www.comingclean-coaching.com** to see when the next group event is and decide if you'd like to join us.

2. If those dates and times don't work, you can check with me about facilitating a group for your facility, company, organization, or retreat center.

3. You can contact me to explore if doing this one-to-one will work best for you.

If you're committed to this process, we can find a way to make it happen. I'd love to meet you and witness the difference Coming Clean and Making AMENDS can make in your life. You can connect with me at **www.comingcleancoaching.com** or penny@wellpower.com.

ACKNOWLEDGMENTS

WRITING A BOOK is a journey made all the more magical because of those I meet along the way. It's also guided by those who have prepared me throughout my life to embrace the unknown.

The creative life may not be the career choice most parents encourage their young to pursue, but my parents, **Nan and Curt Plautz**, knew that ultimately, it was the only choice for me. They've supported my love affair with words and witnessed the wonders that writing have brought into my life.

In many ways, my paternal grandmother's life was defined by her weight and her health challenges, despite her magnificent mind and open heart. Her daughter's life was also impacted by this. My vow to **Dorothy and Marlene Plautz** is that their struggles were not in vain. The shame stops with me. The healing and body confidence begin with me. May all our appetites be honored.

My inner circle of **Everyday Alchemists**, soul sisters who transform the ordinary into the extraordinary, are willing to go wherever life is calling us. Together we've dived deep into joy, power, abundance, and body image. **Kris**, **Teresa**, **Roberta**, **Julia**, **Susan**, **Molly**, **Lynda**, **Reta**, and **Barbi**, your honest feedback, fierce friendship, and profound insights are invaluable to me.

If my first **Coming Clean Coaching Community** wouldn't have taken the leap into cleansing with me, this book wouldn't exist. Because of their commitment to healing and reclaiming their truth, power, and joy, the idea for the love letter to the body was born. Thanks to **Becca**, **Elaine**, **Jan**, **Kellie**, **Kris**, **Susan**, **Sandy**, and **Sun** for trusting me to help you experience your body as sacred and worthy of love.

Thanks to **Robin Colucci** and her team for introducing me to booklet writing and providing step-by-step support from manuscript to marketplace. Thanks to fellow writers **Meghan**, **Jeffifer**, and **Keiko** for sharing a similar journey. May all our books find their way in the world.

Thanks to **Sam Bennett** for introducing me to Robin. Your incomparable knowledge of the workings of the creative mind, experience in transforming that creative expression into cash, precise and profoundly impactful poetry, and genuine affection for your fellow human have inspired me to create daily. I also love that you remind us all that we look really great today.

Thanks to **Jennifer Jas** of *Words With Jas*, editor extraordinaire, who made my writing so much better and immediately became someone I couldn't write without.

Thanks to **Victoria Wolf** of *Wolf Design and Marketing* for working her magic with the cover design and layout.

Thanks to **Polly Letofsky** of *My Word Publishing* for being the midwife to this book baby.

To **Lynda Fletcher** for our weekly Zoom calls where we work out the mysteries of our businesses, our lives, and how to make the world a more creative, welcoming, and inclusive place. Thanks for reminding me to believe the people who believe in me.

To **Kris Vallin** and **Teresa Joy Engel** for Bali and beyond.

To **Fia-Lynn Crandall** and **Makaylah Rogers**, my brilliant Canadian coaches whose insightful, life-changing Scale Naturally program encouraged me to see my weirdness as my edge and align with my natural design. Because of this, I can finally "*peace out*" and capitalize on my quirkiness.

To **Marc David** and **Emily Rosen** and the staff of **The Institute for the Psychology of Eating**, who have created a truly transformative curriculum to help us make peace with food and understand our relationship with our bodies. Becoming a certified eating psychology coach was one of the best investments I've made as well as one of the most healing experiences of my life.

Thanks to **Tom Bonow** for believing in me, trusting my vision, and helping me find the humor in so many things. You've made the Wellpower journey an outrageous adventure.

To **Bob Mitchell**, my fire-fighter fiancé, who keeps my inner fire burning. He regularly relinquishes his favorite chair at the kitchen table so I can turn it into my mobile office and have a room with a spectacular view.

To my **Divine Assistance Team**, my holy host of helpers, angels, guides, and guardians who surprise, delight, and direct my day in the most divine ways. And for reminding me, "*The Universe is always conspiring on my behalf,*" especially when it appears the opposite is true.

And finally to **you, dear brave and beautiful soul**. This loving-yourself business can be brutal. You are worthy of so much love. May you feel it from me in every page of this book.

ABOUT THE AUTHOR

PENNY PLAUTZ helps well-intentioned yet often overwhelmed women reclaim their health, power, and joy.  Clients come to her to help reconcile their relationship with their bodies, get their groove back, and feel good in the skin they are in. Having tried numerous weight loss or self-improvement programs and failing to achieve sustainable results, Penny's clients find her approach disarmingly different. By asking them to *Come Clean* and tell the truth about the life they long to live, she gets to the heart of their discontent. She supports them in taking the necessary steps to rebuild their relationship with their bodies so they can reclaim their personal power and experience more joy.

She began her career in the fitness and hospitality industries. She became an ACE certified fitness instructor and managed hotel and resort health clubs in the Dallas and Fort Worth area of Texas, and in Santa Fe, New Mexico. She also taught fitness classes at corporate fitness centers, community colleges, and destination resorts.

Penny started *Wellpower,* a wellness education company, in 1997 with Tom Bonow. She later owned and operated Transfor*Motion* Studios, a fitness studio and creativity center. Later, she moved to Iowa to oversee operations at a new community college satellite site. She continued to build her coaching practice and work with healers, shamans, and coaches across the United States, Canada, Mexico, England, and Bali.

She is the author of *Wellness Works!* and *Body Confidence from the Inside Out.* Her playful and intuitive approach to health and wellness makes her a popular presenter at destination resorts, recovery centers, and retreats.

Penny holds a bachelor's degree from the University of Northern Iowa, where she spent a year in the National Student Exchange program attending McGill University in Montreal and Université Laval in Quebec City. She also completed graduate courses in Holistic Health at John F. Kennedy University in Orinda, California. She lives in Iowa with her firefighting fiancé and their canine companions.